VINTAGE BLOSSOMS & BLOOMS

Sticker, Color & Activity Book

chartwell books

Quarto

This edition published in 2025 by Chartwell Books,
an imprint of The Quarto Group
142 West 36th Street, 4th Floor
New York, NY 10018 USA
T (212) 779-4972
www.Quarto.com

Contains content originally published as *Embroidery for Everyone* (2021) by becker&mayer! books, and *The Herbalist's Guide for the Sober Curious* (2024), *Crochet Botanicals* (2024), and *Stenciled Book Edges Kit* (2024) by Chartwell Books, imprints of The Quarto Group, 142 West 36th Street, 4th Floor, New York, NY 10018 USA.

10 9 8 7 6 5 4 3 2 1

Chartwell titles are also available at discount for retail, wholesale, promotional, and bulk purchase. For details, contact the Special Sales Manager by email at specialsales@quarto.com or by mail at The Quarto Group, Attn: Special Sales Manager, 100 Cummings Center Suite 265D, Beverly, MA 01915, USA.

ISBN: 978-0-7858-4803-5

Publisher: Wendy Friedman
Publishing Director: Meredith Mennitt
Editor: Jennifer Kushnier
Designer: Brianna Tong
Cover Designer: Sue Boylan

Printed in Huizhou City, China. GP0425.

Peep inside the wonderful
antiquarian world of flowers!

Whether in the densest of cities, or the year's coldest months, or the driest of climates, flowers can be found. Some may even be thriving. With *Vintage Blossoms and Blooms Sticker, Color & Activity Book*, you can take a closer look at the gorgeous blooms all around you—no green thumb required. While you may never get to experience more than a small fraction of the 400,000+ flowering plant species across the globe, you *can* get into the spirit of florists and botanists and partake in some enchanting flower-themed activities.

Set your eyes on the 200+ ornamental stickers featuring all manner of flowers, from blossoms to blooms. Use them to decorate envelopes, gift wrap, letters, scrapbooks, photo albums, and anything else you can think of. There are also inspiring quotes from authors and nature lovers on the backs of the sticker pages for contemplation and relaxation.

To add fun to your free time, flip through the enchanting coloring pages, or test your brain with the variety of original puzzles, mazes, sudoku, trivia, and matching games. Then try your hand at making unique floral drinks; embroidering, crocheting, or arranging flowers; and stenciling book edges—and more!—with the instructions included in the book.

With so many pages to look at, so many things to do, and so much joy to be had in these pages, *Vintage Blossoms and Blooms Sticker, Color & Activity Book* is the perfect book to have on hand when the mood is right. Whether you're a sticker lover, crafter, puzzler, or flower enthusiast, you're sure to find something just for you in this treasure trove of flowery fun!

Match the Flower to the Month!

Just like having a birth stone that's associated with the month you were born, each month also has a flower. There is some variation among sources, but here's what *The Farmer's Almanac* says. See how many you can guess correctly.

answers on the next page

Match the Flower to the Month!

(answer key)

Complete the Picture

solution on page 130

solution on page 130

solution on page 131

solution on page 131

solution on page 132

solution on page 133

solution on page 134

solution on page 135

solution on page 136

"Where flowers bloom,
so does hope."

LADY BIRD JOHNSON

"Even the tiniest flowers can have the toughest roots."

SHANNON MULLEN

See What Flowers

"let us live like flowers
wild and beautiful
and drenched in sun"

ELLEN EVERETT

***I Saw You as a Flower:
A Poetry Collection***

"Flowers are Love's
truest language..."

PARK BENJAMIN, SR.

The Book of the Sonnet

Let's Make Drinks with Flowers!

It might sound strange to "drink flowers," but if you reframe flowers as herbs, then you've probably already had herbal beverages, such as teas or infused sodas. But there's a much bigger botanical world out there! The following pages have a variety of refreshing floral drinks.

But first, here are some ideas for how to dress them up with pretty ice cubes. You can freeze all kinds of different elements in an artful expression for a dramatic, magical drink. Here are some creative ingredients to freeze in your cubes, but note that if you're unsure of what something is, do not use it.

Edible Flowers

Lavender
Chamomile
Thyme flowers
Hawthorn flowers
Broccolini flowers
Violets
Lilacs
Rose petals
Calendula or marigold petals
Nasturtiums
Dandelion petals
Borage (flowers or petals)

Herbs

Mint
Lemon balm
Rosemary
Pine needles

Fruits

Sections of orange, lemon, lime, grapefruit
Pomegranate seeds
Watermelon chunks
Pitted cherries
Blueberries, blackberries, raspberries
Sliced strawberry

Rose Flower Essence

A flower essence is a liquid extract made by infusing flowers in water under sunlight, then typically preserving in alcohol. Rose flower essence is believed to have various emotional and spiritual benefits, including promoting feelings of love, compassion, and inner peace.

What you'll need:

- Handful of fresh organically grown rose petals
- Spring water

What you'll do:

Choose a sunny morning when the roses are at their peak and pick fresh, fragrant petals. Place the petals in a bowl or jar. Fill the bowl with spring water, making sure the petals are completely submerged. Set the bowl outside in a sunny spot where it will receive direct sunlight for at least 4 to 6 hours, preferably longer. This allows the energy of the sun to infuse into the water and the rose petals. Strain the petals from the water using a fine-mesh sieve into a clean glass bottle or jar; label with the contents and date. Store in a cool, dark place for up to several months. Take a few drops directly under the tongue or add them to a glass of water or your herbal drink. You can also add a few drops to bathwater, skincare products, or massage oils.

Dandelion Lemonade

Hello, sunshine! Dandelion lemonade provides a refreshing and unique twist on ordinary lemonades.

What you'll need:

- 4 cups (960 ml) water
- 2 cups (60 g) fresh dandelion petals (remove the green base)
- 1 cup (240 ml) freshly squeezed lemon juice
- ½ cup honey (170 g) or maple syrup (120 ml)
- Ice cubes
- Lemon slices, for garnish

What you'll do:

Bring the water to a boil in a medium saucepan over medium-high heat. Add the dandelion, reduce heat to low, and simmer for 10 to 15 minutes. Strain into a pitcher and let cool slightly. Stir in the lemon juice and honey or maple syrup. Refrigerate until chilled. Serve over ice, garnished with lemon.

Serves 2 to 4

Elderflower & Hibiscus Agua Fresca

This drink combines the delicate floral notes of elderflower with the vibrant, tart flavor of hibiscus, creating a refreshing and visually stunning drink.

What you'll need:

- 4 cups (960 ml) water
- ½ cup (15 g) dried elderflower blossoms (*all* stems removed)
- 2 tablespoons (2 g) dried hibiscus flowers
- ¼ cup (85 g) honey or preferred sweetener
- Juice of 1 lime
- Ice cubes
- Lime slices, for garnish

What you'll do:

In a medium saucepan over medium-high heat, bring the water to a boil, then remove from heat. Add the flowers and steep for 15 to 20 minutes. Strain the infused water into a pitcher, pressing on the flowers to extract flavor. Stir in the honey and lime juice. Refrigerate until chilled. Serve over ice, garnished with lime.

Serves 2 to 4

Lemon Lavender Fizz

The combination of bright lemon citrus and floral lavender creates a balanced and aromatic drink that is both relaxing and revitalizing.

What you'll need:

- ½ cup (120 ml) freshly squeezed lemon juice
- ¼ cup (60 ml) lavender syrup (see Note)
- Ice cubes
- Sparkling water
- 1 or 2 fresh lavender sprigs, for garnish

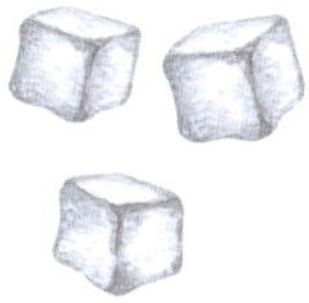

What you'll do:

In a glass, combine the lemon juice and lavender syrup. Fill the glass with ice and top with sparkling water. Stir gently and garnish with fresh lavender.

Serves 1

Note: To make simple syrup, combine ½ cup (120 ml) water and ½ cup (100 g) sugar in a small saucepan. Simmer until the sugar is dissolved. Add ½ cup (15 g) dried culinary lavender buds and simmer 5 minutes more. Remove from heat, allow to cool completely, and strain out the lavender before using. Store in the refrigerator.

Forage Floral Elixir

Florals like rose, lavender, or chamomile impart delicate, aromatic flavors that enhance drinks, providing a unique and soothing experience.

What you'll need:

- 2 cups (480 ml) water
- 1 cup (200 g) sugar
- Handful of edible flowers such as sweet violets, roses, lavender
- 1 tablespoon (15 ml) freshly squeezed lemon juice

What you'll do:

Combine the water and sugar in a small saucepan. Bring to a simmer over medium-low heat, stirring until the sugar is completely dissolved. Remove the syrup from the heat and add the flowers and lemon juice. Cover and steep for 30 minutes to infuse the flavors. Strain through a fine-mesh sieve and let cool completely before transferring it to a clean bottle or jar. Store in the refrigerator for up to 2 weeks. To enjoy, use the syrup as a sweetener for other herbal drinks or mix sparkling water with 1 to 2 tablespoons (up to ¼ cup for a sweeter drink).

Serves 2 to 4

Blossoming Meadow Punch

This stunning punch might just be called "flourishing field of blooms"!

What you'll need:

- 4 cups (960 ml) water
- Handful each of fresh sweet violet flowers, chamomile flowers, lavender, and lemon verbena leaves, plus more for garnish
- 2 cups (480 ml) white grape juice
- ½ cup (170 g) honey
- 1 orange, thinly sliced
- 1 lemon, thinly sliced
- 2 cups (480 ml) sparkling water or club soda
- Ice cubes

What you'll do:

Bring the water to a boil in a medium saucepan over medium-high heat. Add the herbs, reduce heat to low, and simmer for 10 to 15 minutes. Remove from heat and strain into a large punch bowl. Add the grape juice, honey, and citrus slices, stirring to combine. Refrigerate until ready to use. Just before serving, gently stir in the sparkling water and ice. Sprinkle with flowers as garnish.

Serves 8 to 10

Tip: Freeze some of the punch and flowers in a bundt cake pan for a pretty ice ring to place in the punch bowl.

Let's Crochet a Rose!

If you like to crochet—of if you'd like to give it a try—here's an easy project. If you are new to crochet, practice some basic stitches first (see below for the types of stitches and their abbreviations that appear in the pattern). Many yarn and craft shops offer classes, or you can look up video tutorials online.

Crochet flowers work up fast, are a perfect way to use up yarn scraps, and are so colorful and cheery that making them can become almost addictive—but what to do with the finished flowers? Luckily, there are countless possibilities; here are just a few ideas to get you started:

- Customize store-bought (or homemade) clothes and accessories with flower appliques.
- Sew them onto hair clips, barrettes, headbands, or brooches.
- Attach them to earring findings (available at craft stores), or turn them into necklace pendants.
- Sew them together to make a colorful garland.
- Embellish a photo frame with flowers.
- Attach them to green chenille stems and make a bouquet.
- Use them as the finishing touch of gift wrap or create unique gift tags and greeting cards.

What you'll need:

- Worsted acrylic yarn (or yarn of choice)
- G/6 (4mm) crochet hook
- Large yarn needle

Abbreviations

ch	chain or chains
dc	double crochet
sc	single crochet
sl st	slip stitch
YO	yarn over

What you'll do:
Every line starts with the row number in bold, and ends with the stitch count in parentheses. Instructions in square brackets must be repeated the specified number of times before continuing with the remaining instructions of the row (if any).

Finished size: 2" diameter

FIG. A

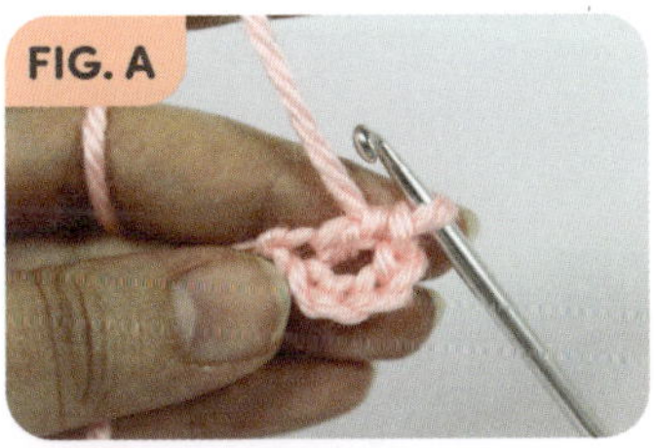

FIG. B

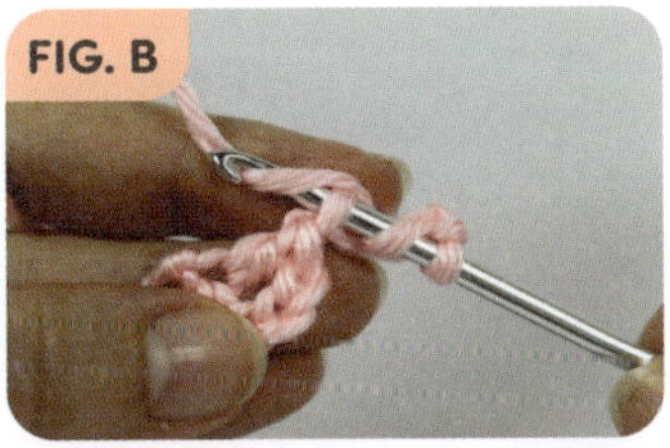

FIG. C

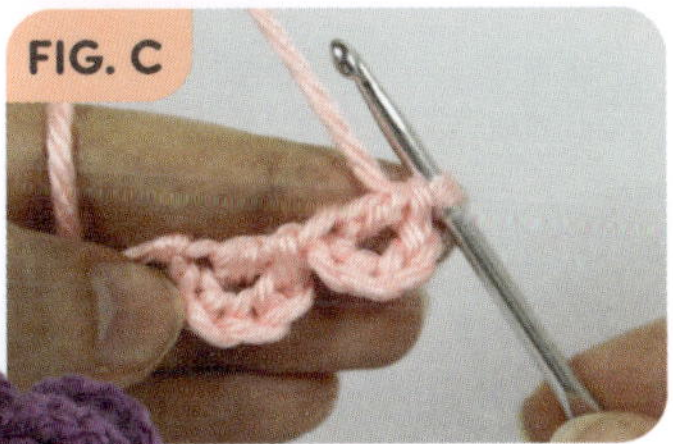

FIG. D

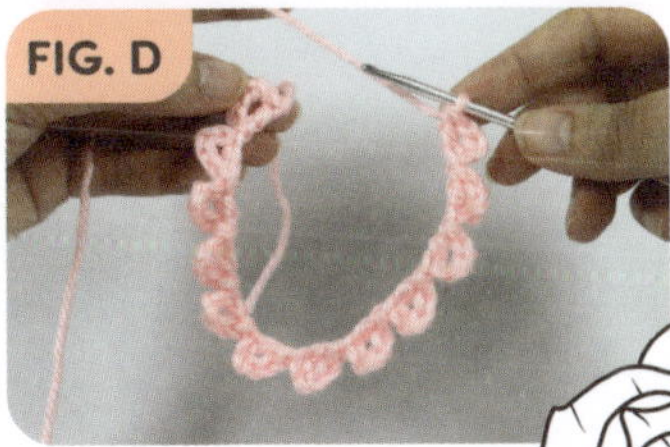

Row 1: With pink yarn, make a slip knot. [Ch 5 and dc in the 5th ch from hook] 12 times **(FIG. A, B, C, D)** (12 chain loops made)

Row 2: Ch 1. Turn your work so you can work into the chain spaces created in row 1: [sc, dc 6, sc] into each loop **(FIG. E, F, G, H)** (12 petals made)
To finish the last petal, sl st into the chain loop **(FIG. I)**, cut yarn leaving a 12" tail, YO and pull end through the last loop on hook.

FIG. E

FIG. F

FIG. G

FIG. H

FIG. I

Roll up the piece so it forms a rose **(FIG. J, K)**. Thread the long yarn end into a needle, turn the rose upside down and stitch through the base several times from multiple directions, to secure the shape **(FIG. L)**.

FIG. J

FIG. K

FIG. L

Caption This!

Fun with Flornithology

Robert Williams Wood, an American physicist and inventor, took the portmanteau of flora (flowers) and ornithology (the study of birds) to the next level with the publication of his 1907 book *How to Tell the Birds from the Flowers and Other Wood-Cuts: A Manual of Flornithology for Beginners.* In it, he describes, in verse and illustration, 49 delightful nature puns, comparing terns to turnips, gnus to newts, larks to larkspur, and pansies to "chim-pansies." In his Author's Apology, below, he references Gray (of Henry Gray's *Anatomy of the Human Body*) and Audubon (of John James Audubon's *The Birds of America*) and makes his apologies to all naturalists.

Not every one is always able
To recognize a vegetable,
For some are guided by tradition,
While others use their intuition,
And even I make no pretense
Of having more than common sense;
Indeed these strange homologies
Are in most flornithologies,
And I have freely drawn upon
The works of Gray and Audubon,
Avoiding though the frequent blunders
Of those who study Nature's wonders.

The Larks. The Larkspur.

You must not make ad-verse remarks,
About my drawing of the Larks.
For, by the minor poet's lore
The Larks—per-pet-ually soar.
While Larkspurs, bordering garden walks,
Are perched securely on their stalks.

The Clover. The Plover.

The Plover and the Clover can be told apart with ease,
By paying close attention to the habits of the Bees,
For en-to-molo-gists aver, the Bee can be in Clover,
While ety-molo-gists concur, there is no B in Plover.

Now try your hand at writing verse to Wood's pictures.

The Auk.

The Orchid.

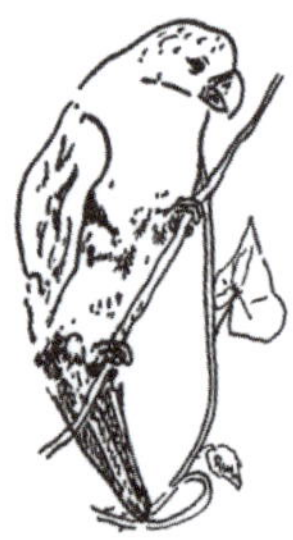

The Blue Mountain Lory.

The Blue Morning Glory.

The Ibis. The 'Ibiscus.

The CowBird. The Cowslip.

Flower Trivia I

How did water lilies, members of the Nymphaeaceae family, get their name?

- O They resemble the juvenile form (nymph) of some water insects.
- O Their petals are laid out in the same pattern as the five stars in the Hyades constellation.
- O They have no root system in the ground and live entirely on water.
- O Their ethereal beauty is reminiscent of a mythical water nymph.

Which of the following is NOT the name of a cactus flower?

- O Organ pipe
- O Prickly pineapple
- O Strawberry hedgehog
- O Christmas

Which flower is associated with the Netherlands?

- O Chrysanthemum
- O Snapdragon
- O Lupine
- O Tulip

Which of the following flowers is NOT a perennial plant (one that comes back every year)?

- O Zinnia
- O Peony
- O Daffodil
- O Purple coneflower

What is one way that flowers propagate?

- O Bulb
- O Seed
- O Rhizome
- O All of the above

Which of the following is NOT one of the four main parts of a flower?

- O Sepal
- O Stamen
- O Uvula
- O Pistil

What does a bluebell flower symbolize?

- O Humility
- O Gratitude
- O Honesty
- O All of the above

answers on page 142

"No matter how chaotic it is, wildflowers will still spring up in the middle of nowhere."

SHERYL CROW

"The petals were voluminous enough to be stirred by the summer breeze, and when they moved, the red, blue and yellow lights passed one over the other..."

VIRGINIA WOOLF

"Kew Gardens"

“Elder, gathered on the last day of April, and affixed to the doors and windows of the house, disappoints designing Witches and protects the inhabitants from their diabolical spells.”

RICHARD FOLKARD, JUN.

Plant Lore, Legends, and Lyrics

"Every flower is a soul
blossoming in nature."

GÉRARD DE NERVAL

"Just living is not enough," said the butterfly, "one must have sunshine, freedom, and a little flower."

HANS CHRISTIAN ANDERSEN

The Complete Fairy Tales

"When you take a flower in your hand and really look at it, it's your world for a moment."

GEORGIA O'KEEFFE

"A rose is a rose is a rose."

GERTRUDE STEIN

"Sacred Emily"

"And the day came
when the risk
to remain tight in a bud
was more painful
than the risk
it took
to blossom."

ANAÏS NIN

"Risk"

Caption This!

Match the Sticker!

answers on page 138

What Is Your *Flower Name?*

Not to be confused with an organism's common name, *binomial nomenclature* is the two-part naming system for all plants, animals, and insects. Developed in 1753 by Swedish biologist Carl von Linne (also known as Linnaeus), it uses Latin to classify all manner of beings. What would *your* flower name be? Match the first letter of your first or last name with the first list of words. Match your birthday with the second list. Perhaps your name will create a lovely new floral species! What would you look like?

Introducing:

____

A *Formosus* (beautiful, well-formed)
B *Nocti* (of the night)
C *Gymno* (naked)
D *Gibbus* (humped)
E *Flavi* (yellow)
F *Alatus* (winged)
G *Hirtus* (hairy)
H *Nitidus* (shining, bright)
I *Gala* (milky)
J *Campanula* (bell-shaped)
K *Incana* (grey)
L *Fasciatus* (striped)
M *Viridi* (green)
N *Cyano* (blue)
O *Echinatus* (prickly, spiny)
P *Alba* (white)
Q *Strepto* (twisted)
R *Suavis* (sweet)
S *Pendula* (weeping, hanging)
T *Setosus* (bristly, shaggy)
U *Virosus* (poisonous, rank)
V *Melano* (black)
W *Reptans* (creeping, crawling)
X *Barbatus* (bearded)
Y *Erythro* (red)
Z *Maculata* (spotted)

1 *Lilium* (lily)
2 *Hydrangea*
3 *Tagetes* (marigold)
4 *Monarda* (bee balm, bergamot)
5 *Ranunculus* (buttercup)
6 *Dianthus* (carnation)
7 *Iris*
8 *Myosotis* (forget-me-not)
9 *Lupinus* (lupine)
10 *Chrysanthemum*
11 *Aquilegia* (columbine)
12 *Clematis*
13 *Delphinium* (larkspur)
14 *Orchidaceae* (orchid)
15 *Tulipa* (tulip)
16 *Zinnia*
17 *Muscari* (grape hyacinth)
18 *Phlox*
19 *Taraxacum* (dandelion)
20 *Papaver* (poppy)
21 *Rosa* (rose)
22 *Hibiscus*
23 *Rudbeckia* (coneflower)
24 *Bellis* (daisy)
25 *Penstemon* (beardtongue)
26 *Cichorium* (chicory)
27 *Antirrhinum* (snapdragon)
28 *Geranium*
29 *Narcissus* (daffodil)
30 *Viola* (viola)
31 *Paeonia* (peony)

Let's Arrange Flowers!

Floristry, or the art of florists, dates back to ancient Egypt, with its preference for the neat and orderly. The ancient Greeks added garlands, wreaths, and cornucopia to the mix, while the Romans pushed their opulence and showiness by adding exotic flowers—and lots of them.

Floristry went into a hibernation of sorts during the Middle Ages, only to bloom again during the Italian Renaissance. From there, artists such as Michaelangelo helped usher in the Baroque style of flower arranging, with its massive yet elegant scale. The Victorians, that prim-and-proper set, began to establish floristry rules, where arrangements were lower in height but high in contrasting color; they also used flowers that conveyed secret meanings.

Today, florists continue to push boundaries and evolve their art, but there are some basic steps to presenting a lovely arrangement—whether you've picked stems from your garden or you bought your bouquet from the supermarket.

What you'll need:

- Vessel
- Sharp scissors or garden shears
- Flower preservative or bleach
- Clear tape, green florists' tape, or chicken wire
- Flowers and greenery

What you'll do:

1. Select an appropriate vase or other vessel. A rule of thumb is that the height of the final arrangement should be at least one and a half

times more than the height of the container. But think about where the arrangement will go: as a coffee table centerpiece, along a wall in an entryway, or on a dining room table. Also consider that a clear vase will require more topping off with water as the days go on. Clean the vessel with soap and water; rinse well.

2. To help support your blooms, tape a grid (like tic-tac-toe) across the top of your vessel; then secure the grid with an extra strip of tape around the lip of the vessel. You can also ball up chicken wire and place it in the bottom.

3. Choose flowers of the same color palette (e.g., all shades of purple) or complementary colors (purple and yellow); or let the colors of the season determine your design. Also consider scent, as noted in The Garden, You, and I (1906): "Heavily scented flowers, such as hyacinths, lemon and auratum lilies, polyanthus narcissus, magnolias, lilacs, and the like, should be avoided." (But this is your arrangement, so do what you like!) When selecting what to include in your arrangement, follow the 3-5-8 rule:

- 3 types of focal flowers (rose, peony, mum, lily, dahlia)
- 5 stems of greenery (myrtle, fern, ivy, grasses, and eucalyptus)
- 8 stems of filler or support flowers (snapdragon, baby's breath, larkspur, ranunculus, carnation, alstroemeria)

4. Cut stems at a 45-degree angle, at least one inch from the bottom, but cut them to different lengths. Remove any leaves that will sit below the water.

5. Add water to the vessel, along with any preservative that came with the bouquet or a couple drops of bleach.

6. Start with your greens; work in a circle around the vessel, crisscrossing the stems along the edges. Add your filler and support flowers, from all angles. Think of building your arrangement as a dome, rather than cramming in the stems like arrows in a quiver. Finally, add your focal flowers.

Match the Garden Tool!

In *Manual of Gardening: A Practical Guide to the Making of Home Grounds and the Growing of Flowers, Fruits, and Vegetables for Home Use* (1910), American horticulturist L. H. Bailey provides comprehensive instructions for building a garden, from the ground up (as it were). He writes, "Persons who followed the entertaining writings of one who called himself Mr. A.B. Tarryer, in "American Garden," will recall the great variety of implements that he advised for the purpose of extirpating his hereditary foes, the weeds." See if you can match Tarryer's weeding tools to their proper names.

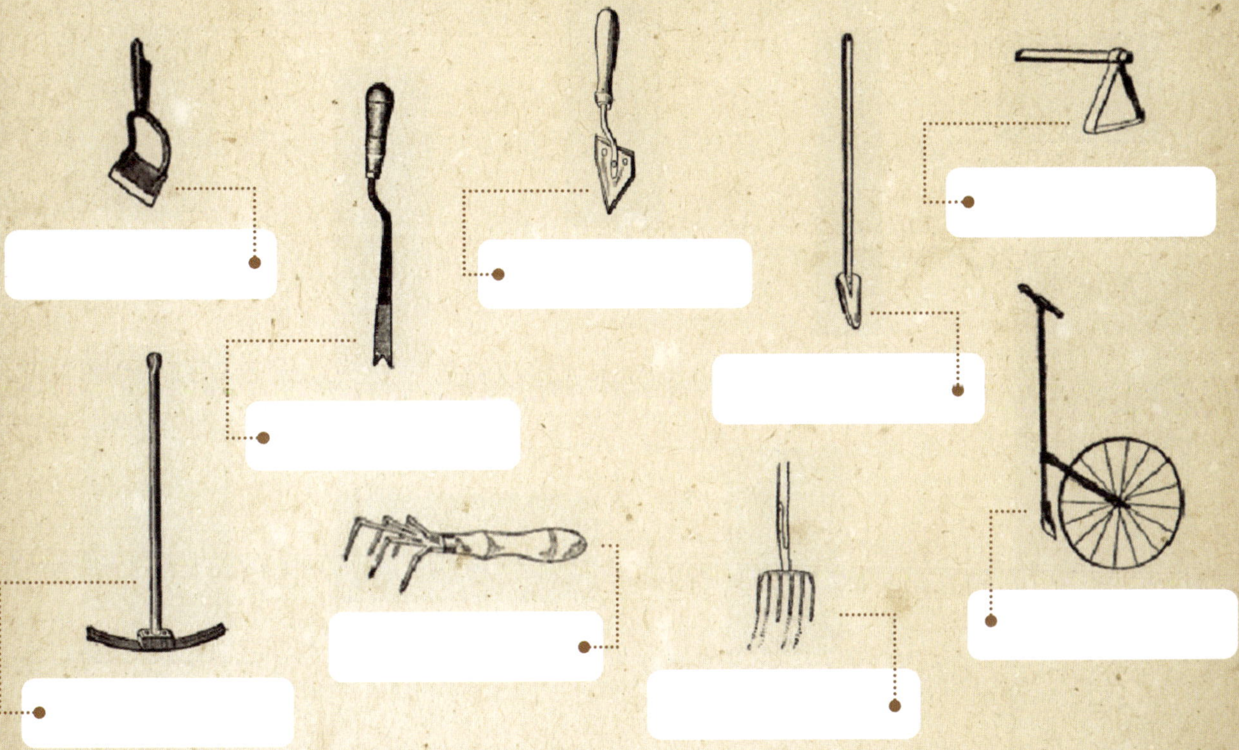

spading fork
single-blade wheel-hoe
common scarifier
hand-weeder
finger-weeder
weed-cutter
weed-spud
long-handled trowel
trowel

answers on the next page

Match the Garden Tool!

(answer key)

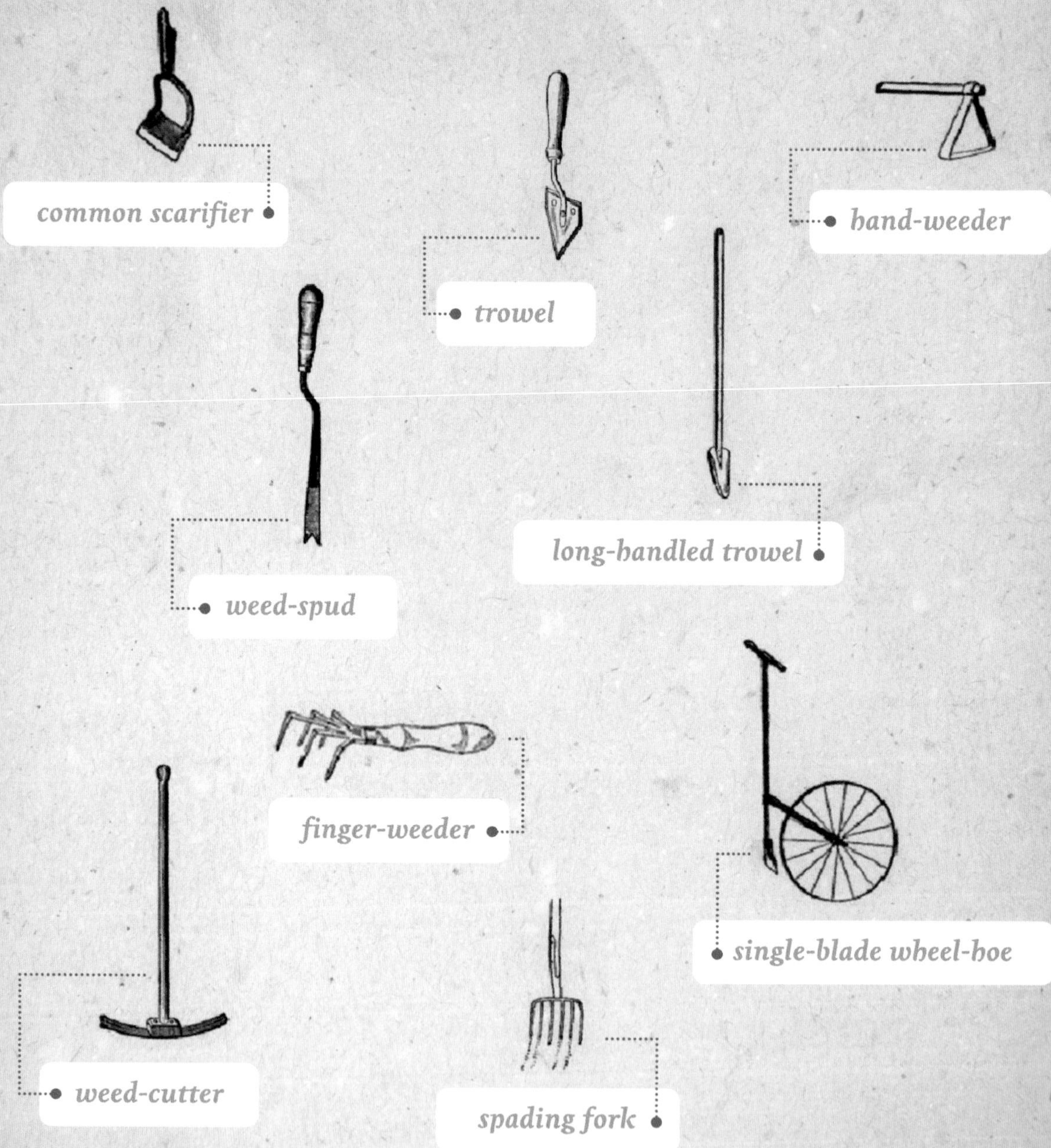

Let's Embroider a Water Lily!

Embroidery is a wonderful way to preserve the beauty of flowers. If you can thread a needle, you can embroider.

What you'll need:

- Water-soluble fabric pen
- Smooth cotton fabric
- Embroidery needle
- Milliner/straw needle (for pistil stitch)
- Embroidery hoop
- 3 colors of 6-stranded, cotton DMC embroidery floss
- Motif

What you'll do:

1. Make a photocopy of the motif and tape it to a window, which will act as a light box. Tape your fabric over the design and trace with the water-soluble pen.

2. Cut thread about 16 inches (40 cm) long. Divide it into the number of strands you need at one end, then slide a finger between the strands and down the length of the thread to separate them.

3. If you're unfamiliar with the types of stitches, search online for how to do straight stitch, backstitch, stem stitch, and pistil stitch, plus how to tie off.

4. **Lily** Use stem stitch to outline the ten uppermost petals with three strands of pink thread and the rest of the petals with four strands. Embroider the lines on the petals as straight stitches with two strands of silver gray and the stamens as pistil stitches with three strands of silver gray.

5. **Leaves** Embroider the lines on the leaves in backstitch and the outlines in stem stitch using four strands of light green.

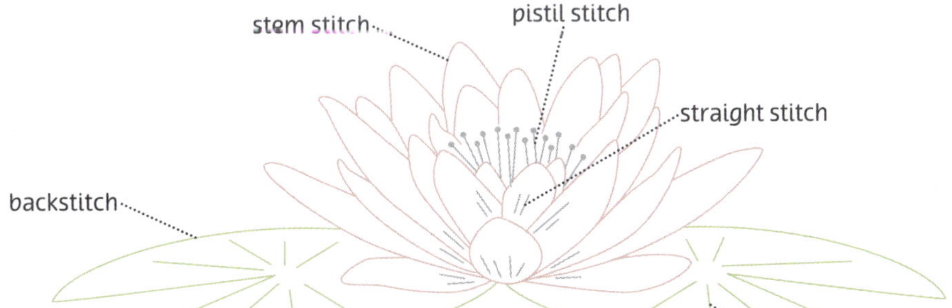
stem stitch
pistil stitch
straight stitch
backstitch
straight stitch

Spot the 15 Differences!

solution on page 137

Complete the Picture

Caption This!

Match the Sticker!

answers on page 140

Sudoku

9	1	6			4		7	2
8			6	2			5	
5					8	9	3	
	6					2		
			2		7			
		5					9	
	9	7	8					3
	8			7	6			9
4	5		1			6	8	7

solution on page 144

Flower Trivia II

Which of the following is NOT a member of the rose family?

- ○ Strawberries
- ○ Quince
- ○ Almonds
- ○ Blueberries

What is the name of a person who studies flowers?

- ○ Entomologist
- ○ Lepidopterist
- ○ Botanist
- ○ Mycologist

Where is the longest-running indoor horticultural indoor flower show in the world?

- ○ Paris, France
- ○ Philadelphia, Pennsylvania
- ○ Tokyo, Japan
- ○ London, England

Which flower is poisonous if eaten?

- ○ Lily of the Valley
- ○ Foxglove
- ○ Oleander
- ○ All of the above

Which flower is NOT a "flower that never sleeps" (aka, a flower that only blooms at night)?

- ○ Sleeping Beauty
- ○ Moonflower
- ○ Night Queen
- ○ Angel trumpet

What was Claude Monet's inspiration for his *Water Lilies* series?

- ○ The Palace of Versailles
- ○ His home in Giverny
- ○ The pond behind Vincent van Gogh's cottage
- ○ La Grenouillère

Which flower is known as the "priceless flower" because it dies almost immediately after being picked?

- ○ Kadupul flower
- ○ Juliet rose
- ○ Saffron crocus
- ○ Gold of Kinabalu orchid

answers on page 143

Sudoku

	3	5	6	7				
4			8	2	9	5		
	8				3		6	
	2				5	8		7
8			2		6			5
3		1	7				2	
	4		9				7	
		2	4	8	7			6
				5	2	4	9	

solution on page 144

Match the Flower to Its Name!

Though naturalist John Berkenhout wrote in 1789, "Those who wish to remain ignorant of the Latin language have no business with the study of botany," there's a lot of fun to be had in the vernacular monikers of plants. While these flower names might sound silly, they're actually quite apt—if you take a good look. See how many you can match.

Love-in-a-Mist ***(Nigella damascena)***
Kangaroo Paws ***(Anigozanthos flavidus)***
Pincushion Flower ***(Scabiosa)***
Bleeding Heart ***(Lamprocapnos spectabilis)***
Shrimp Plant ***(Justicia brandegeeana)***
Drumsticks ***(Craspedia globosa)***
Goat's Beard ***(Aruncus dioicus)***
Kiss Me Over the Garden Gate ***(Persicaria orientalis)***
Lady's Slipper ***(Cypripedium acaule)***
Red Hot Poker ***(Kniphofia)***
Butter and Eggs ***(Linaria vulgaris)***
Lobster Claw ***(Heliconia)***

answers on the next page

Match the Flower to Its Name!

(answer key)

Goat's Beard

Love-in-a-Mist

Red Hot Poker

Bleeding Heart

Lobster Claw

Shrimp Plant

Kangaroo Paws

Pincushion Flower

Kiss Me Over the Garden Gate

Lady's Slipper

Drumsticks

Butter and Eggs

Let's Stencil a Book Edge!

Dating back to tenth century England, the tradition of fore-edge painting describes all the activities related to embellishing the paper edges of a book. The practice reached the peak of its popularity in the second half of the 17th century but has seen a resurgence in popularity in the 21st. It's a lovely (and easy) way to add a touch of antiquarian finery to your bookshelf. Here's how you can create your very own collector's editions of your favorite books.

What you'll need:

- Book
- Sheets of paper or craft paper
- Painter's or washi tape
- Microfiber cloth
- A small dish to hold paint
- 2 book clamps or C-clamps
- Acrylic paint(s)
- Sponge dabber or foam brush
- Vinyl adhesive stencil (available online, or create your own with a Cricut machine)

What you'll do:

1. Remove the dust jacket from the cover (if there is one). Wrap the front and back covers using sheets of paper and tape to protect them from the paint.

2. Secure the book with the clamps so that the pages are as tightly compressed as possible to give you an even surface to paint on (Fig. 1). Wipe the edge of the book with the cloth to remove dust.

Fig. 1

Fig. 2

3. Position the stencil on the front edge in the correct position, press well so it adheres, and remove the clear transfer tape layer (Fig. 2).

4. Using a dry sponge dabber or foam brush, dab on small amounts of paint at a time to avoid paint bleeding beneath the stencil (Fig. 3). Try not to saturate the page; you can add more layers or colors with a light touch after the first layer/color dries.

Fig. 3

5. Allow your project to dry completely, at least one hour.

6. Remove the clamps, then carefully open the front and back covers to loosen the stencil. Beginning at the top or bottom edge, slowly pull off the stencil. Gently wiggle and maneuver groups of pages to loosen them, then flip or fan through small sections at a time, loosening up more pages as you go.

7. Remove the paper wrapping, replace the dust jacket, and admire your beautiful new book.

Let's Make Vintage Paper Flowers!

The Victorians loved a good paper craft, they loved flowers, and they really loved paper flowers as decoration. True to Victorian form, some flowers were elaborate, but you can create a simple rose with just a couple supplies.

What You'll Need:

- Sheet of colorful paper (such as those on the next couple pages)
- Scissors
- Glue or hot glue gun

What You'll Do:

1. Cut out a scalloped circle around the edge of the paper. (A line is on the pages for reference, but you can cut your own.)

2. Cut a scalloped spiral from the outer edge to the center, keeping the strip at least ½-inch wide. Leave a small circle at the center, where you'll add glue at the end.

3. Starting from the outside edge, start rolling up the paper, making your way to the center. It's okay if it's tight right now.

4. Put your finger through the center, so it's touching the bottom of the flower, and allow the spiral to unfurl a bit until the "petals" look good to you.

5. Add a dab of glue in the center, pressing toward the bottom of the flower, and allow to dry.

Tip: Add a bit of florist's wire to the flower, and you can attach it to wreaths, vases, branches, frames, or turn a bunch into a bouquet.

Caption This!

maze on page 8

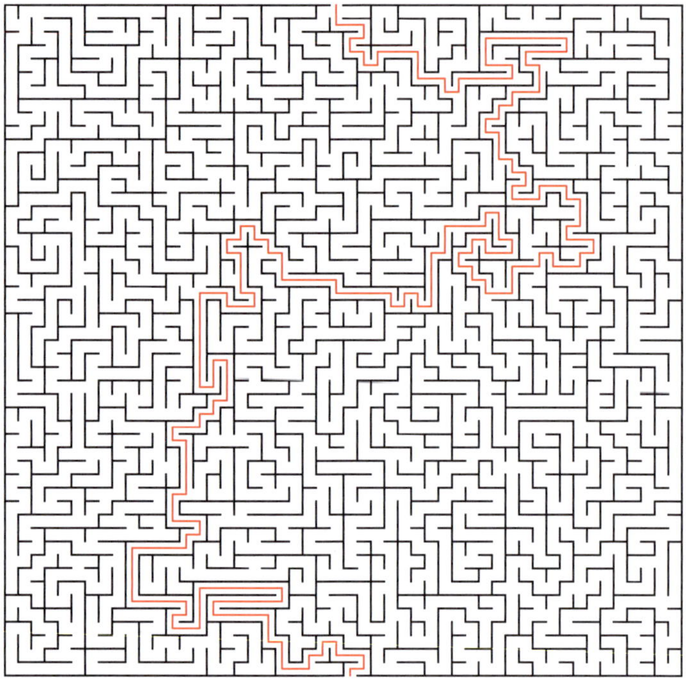

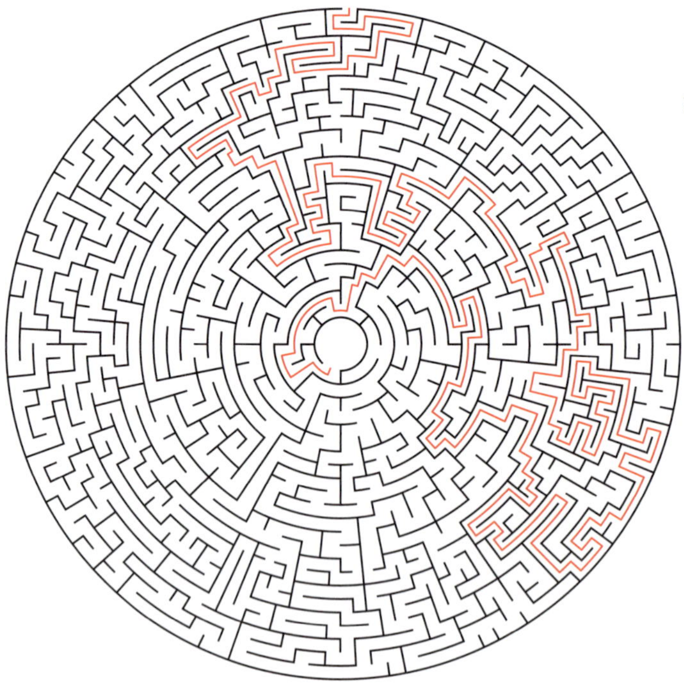

maze on page 9

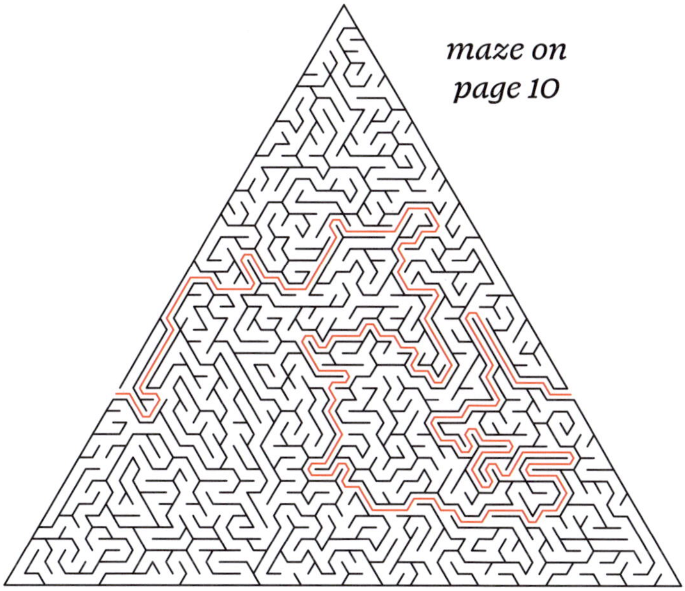

maze on page 10

maze on page 11

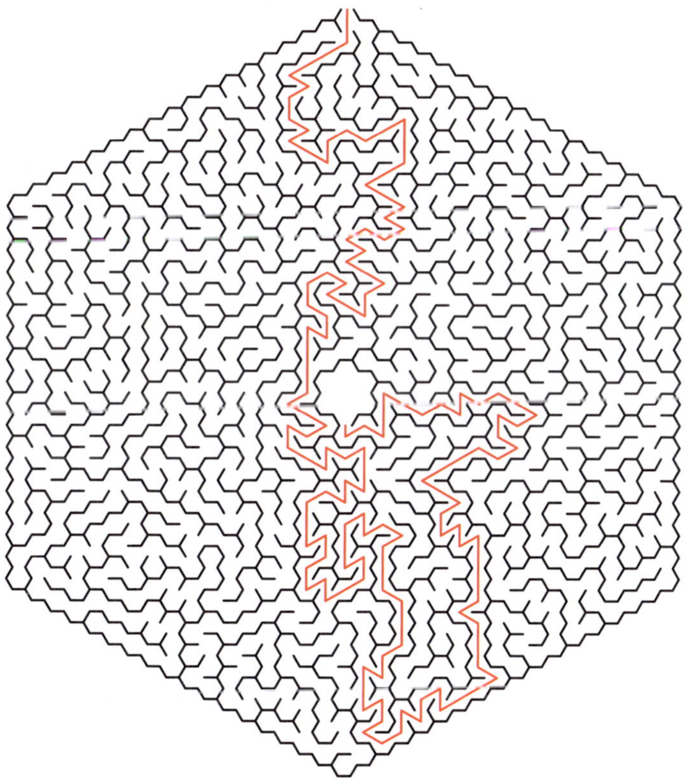

maze on page 12

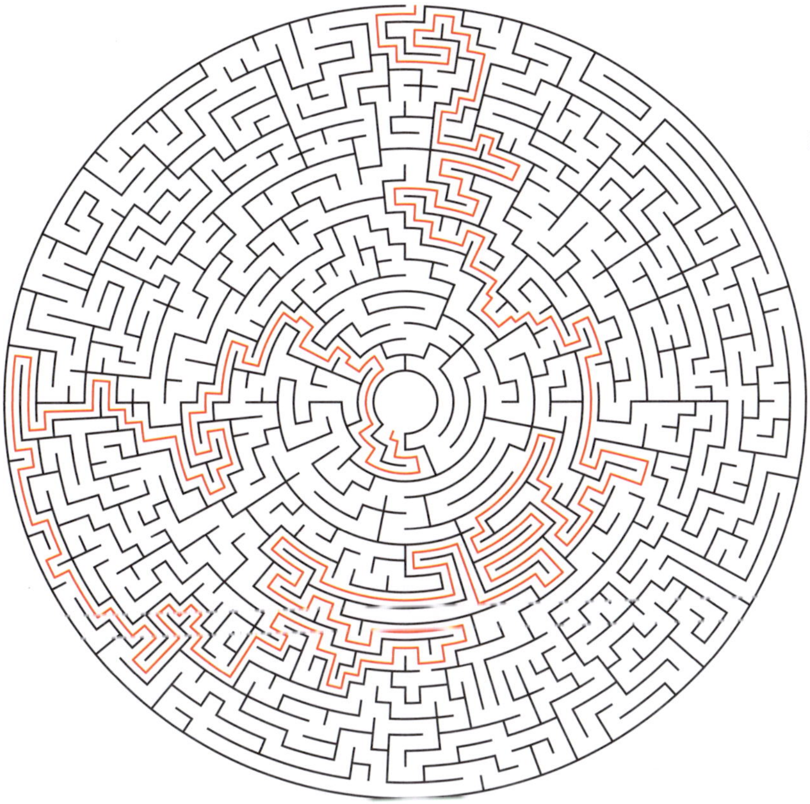

maze on page 13

maze on page 14

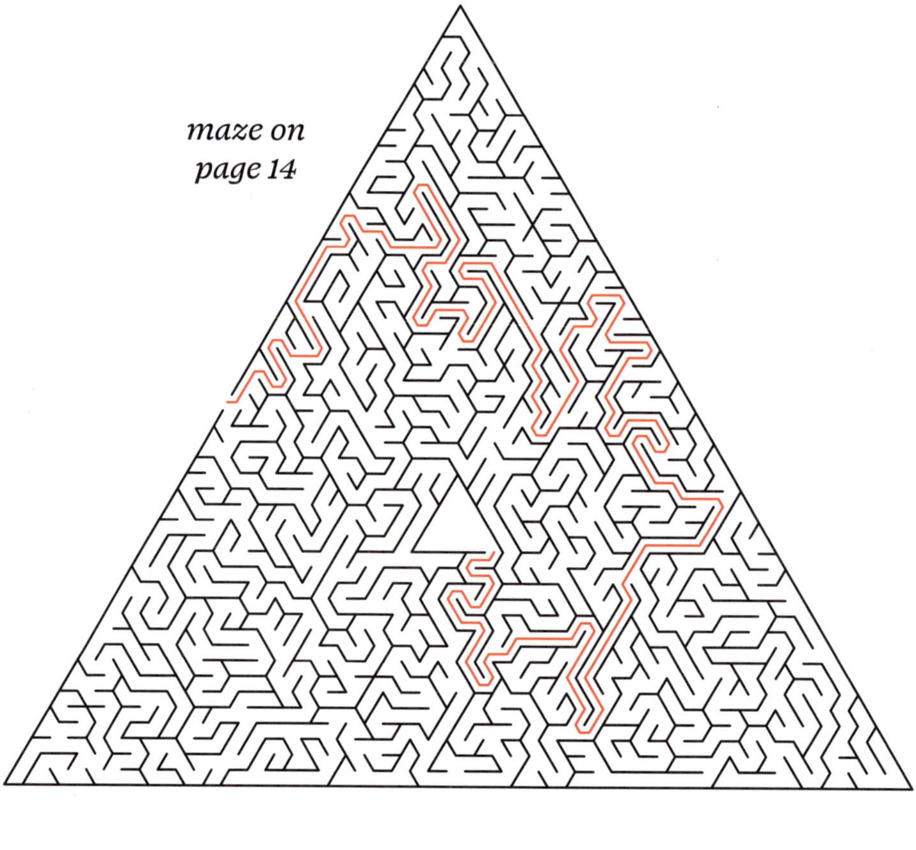

maze on page 15

maze on page 16

Spot the 15 Differences! *(answer key)*

puzzle on page 110

Match the Sticker!

(answer key)

sticker on
page 62
sticker on
page 55
sticker on
page 26
puzzle on page 98

Match the Sticker!

(answer key)

sticker on page 86
sticker on page 90
sticker on page 59
puzzle on page 114

Flower Trivia I *(answer key)*

How did water lilies, members of the Nymphaeaceae family, get their name?

- ○ They resemble the juvenile form (nymph) of some water insects.
- ○ Their petals are laid out in the same pattern as the five stars in the Hyades constellation.
- ○ They have no root system in the ground and live entirely on water.
- ✓ Their ethereal beauty is reminiscent of a mythical water nymph.

Which of the following is NOT the name of a cactus flower?

- ○ Organ pipe
- ✓ Prickly pineapple
- ○ Strawberry hedgehog
- ○ Christmas

Which flower is associated with the Netherlands?

- ○ Chrysanthemum
- ○ Snapdragon
- ○ Lupine
- ✓ Tulip

Which of the following flowers is NOT a perennial plant (one that comes back every year)?

- ✓ Zinnia
- ○ Peony
- ○ Daffodil
- ○ Purple coneflower

What is one way that flowers propagate?

- ○ Bulb
- ○ Seed
- ○ Rhizome
- ✓ All of the above

Which of the following is NOT one of the four main parts of a flower?

- ○ Sepal
- ○ Stamen
- ✓ Uvula
- ○ Pistil

What does a bluebell flower symbolize?

- ○ Humility
- ○ Gratitude
- ○ Honesty
- ✓ All of the above

trivia on page 48

Flower Trivia II *(answer key)*

Which of the following is NOT a member of the rose family?

- ○ Strawberries
- ○ Quince
- ○ Almonds
- ☑ Blueberries

What is the name of a person who studies flowers?

- ○ Entomologist
- ○ Lepidopterist
- ☑ Botanist
- ○ Mycologist

Where is the longest-running indoor horticultural indoor flower show in the world?

- ○ Paris, France
- ☑ Philadelphia, Pennsylvania
- ○ Tokyo, Japan
- ○ London, England

Which flower is poisonous if eaten?

- ○ Lily of the Valley
- ○ Foxglove
- ○ Oleander
- ☑ All of the above

Which flower is NOT a "flower that never sleeps" (aka, a flower that only blooms at night)?

- ☑ Sleeping Beauty
- ○ Moonflower
- ○ Night Queen
- ○ Angel trumpet

What was Claude Monet's inspiration for his *Water Lilies* series?

- ○ The Palace of Versailles
- ☑ His home in Giverny
- ○ The pond behind Vincent van Gogh's cottage
- ○ La Grenouillère

Which flower is known as the "priceless flower" because it dies almost immediately after being picked?

- ☑ Kadupul flower
- ○ Juliet rose
- ○ Saffron crocus
- ○ Gold of Kinabalu orchid

trivia on page 117

puzzle on page 116

9	1	6	3	5	4	8	7	2
8	7	3	6	2	9	1	5	4
5	2	4	7	1	8	9	3	6
7	6	8	9	3	5	2	4	1
1	4	9	2	8	7	3	6	5
2	3	5	4	6	1	7	9	8
6	9	7	8	4	2	5	1	3
3	8	1	5	7	6	4	2	9
4	5	2	1	9	3	6	8	7

puzzle on page 118

1	3	5	6	7	4	9	8	2
4	7	6	8	2	9	5	1	3
2	8	9	5	1	3	7	6	4
6	2	4	1	9	5	8	3	7
8	9	7	2	3	6	1	4	5
3	5	1	7	4	8	6	2	9
5	4	3	9	6	1	2	7	8
9	1	2	4	8	7	3	5	6
7	6	8	3	5	2	4	9	1